NATIONAL GEOGRAPHIC

D0503674

When a Storm Comes

Kate McGough

Look at this field.
There are no trees or bushes.
There is no grass.
What will happen when a storm comes?

When a storm comes, the wind can blow the soil away.
The rain can wash the soil away.
The wind and rain can move the soil to another place.
This is called erosion.

Sometimes people do things that cause erosion, too.
Look at this field.
A farmer is clearing the land to plant seeds in the soil.

There are no trees or bushes in the field.
There is no grass.
What will happen when a storm comes?

When a storm comes, the soil washes away. Without soil, the crops can't grow.

But farmers can stop erosion.
Look at this field.
The farmer has left some trees and bushes in the field.
The trees and bushes will keep the soil
from washing away.

11

When a storm comes, the rain will soak into the earth.
Only a little bit of soil will wash away.
The field is safe and the crops will grow.